INEVITABLE WHAT

INEVITABLE WHAT

SARAH LYN ROGERS

ILLUSTRATED BY
SIRIN THADA

Copyright © 2016, 2017 by Sarah Lyn Rogers.
All rights reserved. Printed in the United States of America.

Second printing 2017.
First published 2016 by Sad Spell Press.

Sarah Lyn Rogers
www.sarahlynrogers.com

Cover, design, and illustrations by Sirin Thada Studio.
www.sirinthadastudio.com

The text of this book is set in Palatino.

The origins of poetry are clearly rooted in obscurity, in secretiveness, in incantation, in spells that must at once invoke and protect, tell the secret and keep it.

— Mary Ruefle, *Madness, Rack, and Honey*

CONTENTS

NEW MOON RITUAL	1
LORE	3
TACIT	5
RAT RACE	7
CHURCH LATIN	8
DROWNING OUT A PUJA WITH NORAH JONES	9
APATHY SPELL	11
"SLEEPING LADY PLATE," 1976	13
AMBITIEUSE	15
BENIGN	17
SPIDER HANDS	19
VANISHING ACT	21
THE SOMNAMBULIST	23
"YOU CAN NEVER QUITE FORGIVE" (148).	25
SADNESS RITUAL	27
BEGGAR WOMAN SPELL	29
LARGO CHIADO	31
JULY 2014	33
DRONES	35
GREY	37

NEW MOON RITUAL

Prepare no circle. Leave the wick unlit.
To let go, you need only cut some strings.

Red for the first muse of your quiet youth:
cigars, mohawk, machismo in a skirt.

Green for the wanderlusting polyglot:
soft-voiced schemer, the sudden musician.

Black for the mentor who meant more: mother
figure: old school punk with a PhD.

All women you placed on a pedestal—
a gilded tower. You spoke from the ground

until you didn't, your reverence deadened
by business lingo, "breach of contract," "you

do not make art," absence despite countless
invitations. Exposure to ego

conjured ego: white for your ignorance,
the pettiness of settling a score.

Clip these ghosts. Repeat the following:
They are nothing. I am nothing, too.

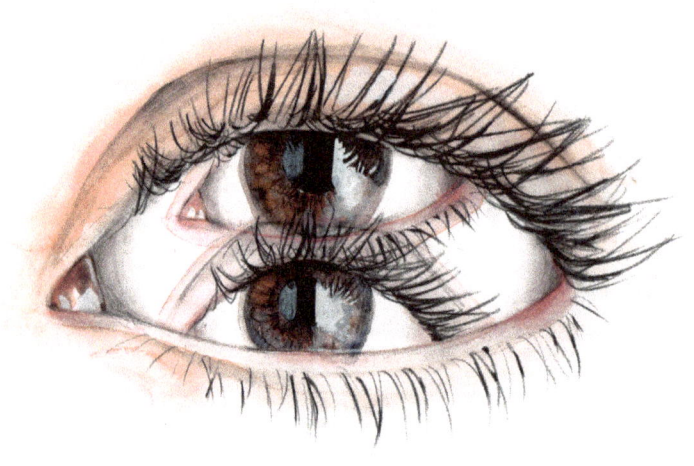

LORE

woke with an opal in your hand
after a night of restlessness

you'd dreamed the usual things:
flight, a chase, sounds that

should have been words—still
empty-handed when the man

who always leaves left.
morning peeled up the shades

of your eyes. you found
the bauble like a stone to skip

cupped in your knuckles.
what startled you was the weight

the sense of anything
pushing back

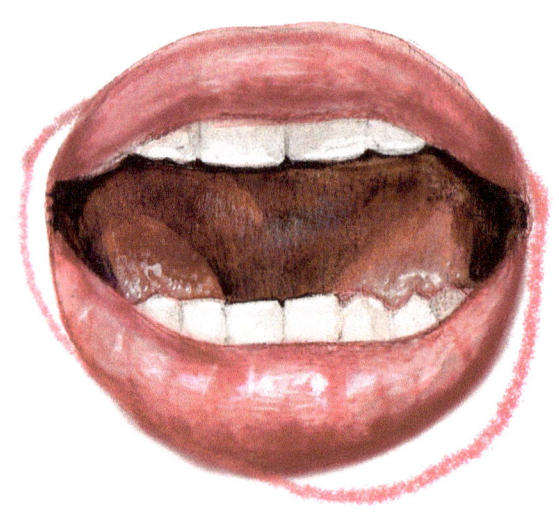

TACIT

like pushing a stone upslope sometimes
this need to speak, to explain

exactly what we mean when nouns
like trinkets deep in a pocket

refuse to come forth and we must
scrounge for change

for the next closest thing:
the lint wrapped around our intent

the inevitable *what* stings—
hot zap of misunderstanding

glitch

in the language we have shared
in our lifetimes before words

RAT RACE

Our housecat decimates
a raspberry
while I (hands pruning
in Palmolive foam)
ponder the tameable wild.

Riding past, a pair
atop a tandem bicycle
reads like a commercial
for wrist leashes
      taupe upholstery
            the champagne colored cars
prescribed to persons
of reasonable means.

We make meaning from this
procession of wants:
      the house one can afford
           Wwa tasteful coat of paint—
not what stokes a fire in the mind
not what a taskless hunter's craze creates.

I ache
to make something
of substance

goaded by the knowing glance
of a sweet, primeval
creature in my kitchen
both of us domesticated;
framed.

CHURCH LATIN

Sonam, he knew it would be there,
high up the mountainside, through
dry brush and brown needles, past
an old woman's shack just by
the lone cow grazing before
a metal gate, along
the slim dirt path, beyond
thicker clusters of pines, up
to the rock his mind recognized
where there'd be a cave, he knew,
for the goddess of music.

He'd been led by a dream
the monks have forbidden him to tell
(except to them, of course).

It is a *secret dream*
and the unenlightened stay where they're kept:
in the dark, as ever. In the dark.

DROWNING OUT A PUJA WITH NORAH JONES

Not that I don't care for the low drone
of those long horns carried by monks
drums sounded by hooks
trumpet notes racing up invisible stairs, or the

crash   crash   crash   crashcrash
crash   crash   crash   crashcrash

Not sure whether this smoke, these high tones
are clearing bad energy after a tragedy
or averting one. Tshering said
when he built his new house he needed

pujas at each stage of the process,
always on auspicious days (of course).
Preventing bad luck required a blessing
from a virgin under the age of eighteen.

What if you're fresh out of those, I asked.
We had to put out an ad, he said.

crash   crash   crash   crashcrash
crash   crash   crash   crashcrash

While my neighbors wail, I wash dishes.
My ritual is this: orange rubber gloves,
the hottest water our heater can muster
swathing the kitchen in steam.

When I clean, I light incense
which might be sacrilegious
but to me means purposefulness.

Above my neighbors' holy cacophony
my aural field is "adult contemporary"
tickled ivories and cool-cat upright bass.

In my chamber of steam and smoke
the mind empties, hands complete the task.
Not sacred, this cleansing. Still essential:

small-scale chaos made pure

APATHY SPELL

Maybe no one will want it: holes
in the floorboards you patched

with cardboard and tape, defending
your fortress against a different rat,

peeling paint on cold cement walls
gouged and oily with handprints

brown-stained caulking on the tile
silverfish, pill bugs, windows

that never quite close. A home
another pair might find demeaning.

Maybe someone *would* want it
for the price—the reason you have it

why you're not, like the other chillips,
somewhere that seems like "Shangri-La."

Though you have no control
weigh the outcomes:

Keeping the known, with its flaws.
A chance to improve by uprooting.

You will deal with whatever.

And so it shall be or better.

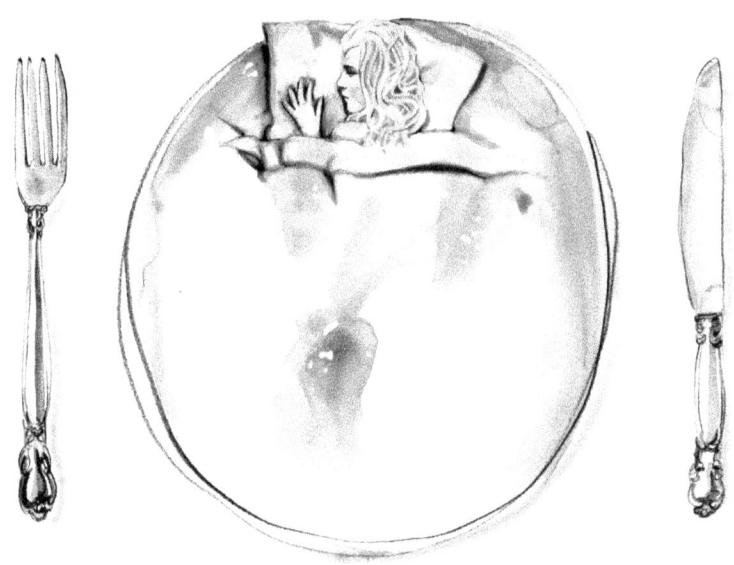

"SLEEPING LADY PLATE," 1976

Porcelain person
are you peaceful on the plate
dreaming downy mashed potatoes?

Or do the rumpled sheets reveal your restlessness?

You must be stone-cold
tucked in glossy iridescence
alone.

Is this a life? Awakening under steak?
The ever-present threat of saucy stains?

Your hair—spaghetti strands
your fragile, bone-white hand
this figure face-down on two smooth pillows

charms me
with...false? serenity

the glint of glaze
and how your sleeping eyes
won't meet my gaze.

AMBITIEUSE

For you
I am long out of print

a dense paperback
approved by your mother—

the cover tattered
neutral colored

smothered
unlike others:

self-affirming codes of conduct
    your annotated textbooks
        your diaries—rewritten, always right.

Cleaned "clutter" and
junked me. I

smoldered
in the stack of books you burned.

I know at least *one* word
you never learned.

BENIGN

it wasn't four glasses of water
or the man's hand applying
pressure and hot jelly
on my bladder

not the loud and lengthy horse piss
certainly heard through the door
nor the bare-assed shuffle
to the table

not prognosis: ping pong ball in my body
fallopian tagalong threatening rupture

no

kept my composure until now:
this hundred-year-old reel in black and white
a sweet-faced thing that doesn't know it's dead
it wags its tail and yawns, a century gone

repeat
repeat

the last Tasmanian tiger

SPIDER HANDS

When the leaves changed
I drew the blinds
and buried you deep
where the skeletons dance

When wind chill whips
my naked nape
I feel your fingers
padding softly:

Spider hands crept up the neck
and plucked the strings

Spine-tingling vibrations
set my blood abuzz

You quivered;
I froze

I love the winter chill, but, oh,
how you beckon, Mr. Bones

Sometimes, bit by tiny bit,
I unearth you

Carefully
so as not to thaw

VANISHING ACT

Alarm-clock puppeteer, you do your worst.
String up the quilt and kick me, quick, awake
into the fog of maybe-still-asleep
wherein I kiss my lover's static face—
remote from me, eyes inward-turned to dreams—

then drive home under glare of stale moonbeams.
Sheets hiss a sinister goodbye and I
am apt to wrap my sleepy self again
in satiny embrace to brace against
the wee-hours air in Winter, Fall, or Spring.

I hate you as a necessary thing
but love what your necessity involves.
It matters little that I must arise
at two when at midnight the world dissolves.

THE SOMNAMBULIST

Between my sleeping body and your bed
the silent drive, the moonlight-painted sky
ferry you homeward to your dog-eared books.
Sonatas, origami, your pursuits—
proficiencies you glean while I'm asleep—
are lullabies. Brain shrouded thick with stars
and seedlings of your plans, you slumber then:
your eyelids soft, headphones about your ears
papers and pages taut between your hands.

These images are fancied from your words—
my daydream of descriptions of your nights.
That scholar-space inhabited by you
is womblike, liminal, not for the harsh
confounding light or scrutiny of day
(*not for me, either*, I acknowledged then
with chest swelled for my mute supporting role:
the genius's kind wife out of the way
for art, invention, things of great import).

Two glasses by your sink, both ringed with wine—
they drained to white the roses in my cheeks.

"YOU CAN NEVER QUITE FORGIVE" (148).

Inside a book your lover lends, you'll spy
a hard-creased upper corner, bottom too.
The framed page begs attention from your eye—
the author's words, highlighted, outline you.
That *tiny hate* from late-requited love
cuts through the text—the phrase lingers, it stains.
You stomach every implication of
this ink you picture oozing in his veins.
With kisses, siphon it. Time is the cure
the novel's hero had no chance to know.
Your actions, heroine, will reassure
the one whose borrowed words have stirred you so.
Return the book of secrets. On a whim
unbend the page reminding you of him.

SADNESS RITUAL

It is given [so] that you will hold it.

You, vessel shaped like an answer.
Keeper of sadness, its mistress
alchemist to stomach it and yield

gold. Anything other than this
tense second-guessing, infiltrating
every word you say or consider.

Every stilted gesture. What
starts with others often
ends with you:

vessel holding his sorrow
vessel holding yourself.

BEGGAR WOMAN SPELL

On the praça, an old woman walks
with arresting confidence—
back rigid, eyes eagle-sharp
as though in slow motion

a different plane of time
from the crowd around her
parting like smoke. That's
when she casts her glamour

lifting her cane to the air
stooping, hunchbacked
beckoning for change
in the whine of a stray cat.

LARGO CHIADO

The man in the hat, he sits.
He's been sitting for a hundred years—at least

in my imagination. The facts
are these: he is bronze, not brawny

in a chair at the Café Brasileira
where he was built in 1988.

Ankle fused to knee, arm raised
as if ready to speak, he

watches passing people scuff the cobble
place cigarettes between his fingers

pose on him for pictures
and never says a word, except at night.

He has no horse, no gun, no sword—
only one hopefully-good book.

That man in the hat, he stands
as a different kind of figurehead.

Surname: "Person." Man of many nyms
who stuffed his words inside a wooden trunk.

A quiet guy—
a flâneur, not a fighter.

JULY 2014

How many gold leaf Marys with a baby
can a person see before they look the same?

Trick question—it slowly dawns,
like the knowledge that you are not wanted here

crowding the streets, museums, restaurants
the locals no longer frequent. You are

an annoyance. Slow your pace at the station
and a woman shoots a breath into your neck

hot, loud, full of malice. *You people*, it says
don't belong here. In line, everyone hovers

as you count your foreign change to the teller
who told you the total in a mumble.

Set down your coins and you hear it again—
the battle cry, hot sigh that sails like a bullet.

You cannot control whether others
resent your presence. Still,

this is better than being killed
for that, someone's perception

that you are not entitled to space,
like the conflict on the news every night.

There, what sails like a bullet is a bullet,
or bullets, filled with tiny skin-slicing darts.

Cruelty is crafty, you learn.
Those with most of the guns

and all of the food
can play the victim, too.

When you wake in the morning, flesh raw
from fresh mosquito bites, you are angry.

In sleep you must yield all control
to hidden menaces. Your vulnerable body.

At least you wake up.

DRONES

My father, whose fifteen-year hobby has been
conservative windbag idolatry

despite his blue-collar job, two-foot bong
and lack of liquid assets

is obsessed by tiny helicopters, like many
middle-aged men suddenly.

For weeks he's perfected smooth figure-eights
over the heads of his dogs, taking tips

from retirees, the delighted society
of those who "go fly" at the park

who know this machine the way men perform knowing—
down to the specs, model numbers, speeds and dials.

A harmless hobby. There is nothing
subjective about it.

He wants to instruct. I hold the remote
like I'm six, and a boy.

This is the way you control it. When it dies
replace the battery. I think about bombs

falling from drones and give the object
too much power. *It's okay*, he says.

If anything bad happens, just kill the throttle.

GREY

Through the glass pane: sky
muted as my impulses.
And yet expansive.

Season of soul-drought
I crack for want of water.
Will you never end?

In the wings, blue clouds
beckon, *Now*. I will answer.
I will call the rain.

AUTHOR ACKNOWLEDGMENTS

For my sweetheart, parents, teachers, and my friends; for everyone who's brought a little magic to my life.

Thank you to the following journals, in which these poems previously appeared—some in different forms:

- *3Elements Review* — "Rat Race"
- *Caesura* — "'You can never quite forgive' (148)."
- *Chantarelle's Notebook* — "Spider Hands"
- *Cosumnes River Journal* — "'Sleeping Lady Plate,' 1976"
- *DMQ Review* — "Drones"
- *Three: An Anthology of Flash Nonfiction* — "Grey"

Much gratitude to Catch Business and Sad Spell Press for publishing the first edition.

A NOTE ABOUT THE AUTHOR

Sarah Lyn Rogers is a Pushcart-nominated writer, the former Fiction Editor for *The Rumpus*, and the Editorial Director for Society of Young Inklings. For more of her work, visit sarahlynrogers.com.

A NOTE ABOUT THE ILLUSTRATOR

Sirin Thada is an artist, illustrator, and designer based in New York City. For more of her work, please visit her portfolio at sirinthadastudio.com.

www.ingramcontent.com/pod-product-compliance
Lightning Source LLC
Chambersburg PA
CBHW062106290426
44110CB00022B/2728